EYE OPENERS

12/99
MSC

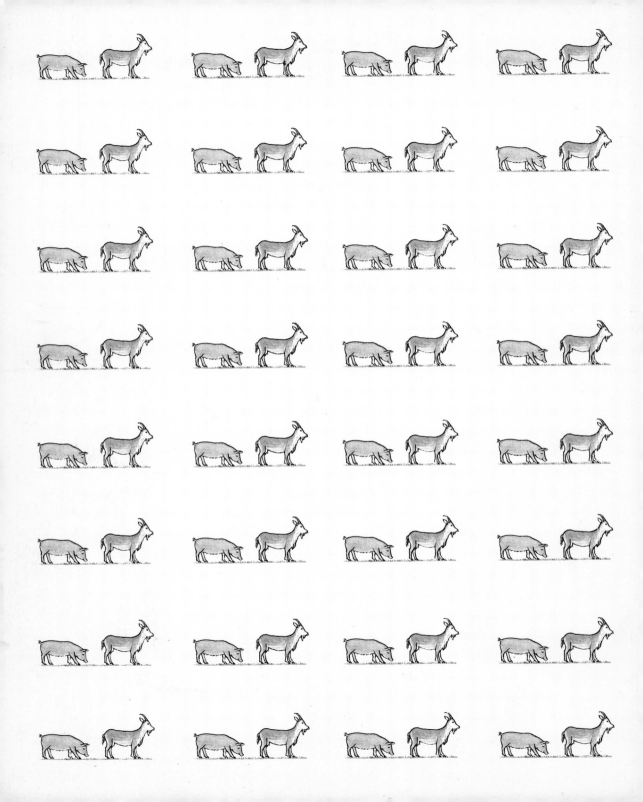

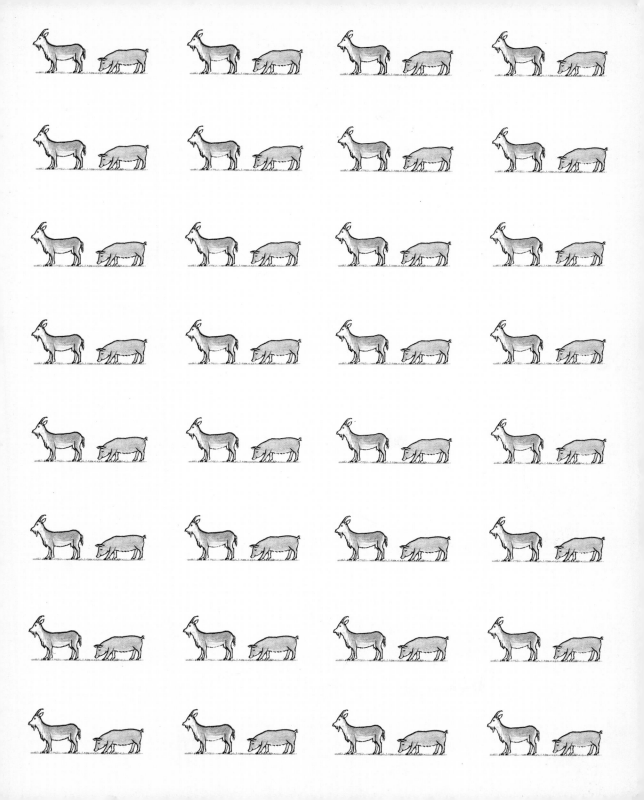

www.dk.com

Senior Editor Jane Yorke
Editor Dawn Sirett
Senior Art Editor Mark Richards
Art Editor Jane Coney
Production Marguerite Fenn

Photography by Philip Dowell
Additional Photography by Michael Dunning
(pages 10-11 and 14-17)
Illustrations by Martine Blaney,
Dave Hopkins, and Colin Woolf
Animals supplied by Ashdown Forest Farm,
Hackney City Farm, Horton Park Farm,
and Surrey Docks Farm

Eye Openers ®

First published in Great Britain in 1991
by Dorling Kindersley Limited,
9 Henrietta Street, London WC2E 8PS
Reprinted 1991, 1993 (twice), 1995
First paperback edition, 1999

Text copyright and photography
(pages 4-5, 10-11, and 14-17) copyright © 1991
Dorling Kindersley Limited, London
Photography (pages 6-9, 12-13, and 18-21)
copyright © 1991 Philip Dowell

A CIP catalogue record for this book is
available from the British Library.

ISBN 0-7513-5950-5

Reproduced by Colourscan, Singapore
Printed in China

EYE OPENERS
Farm Animals

London • New York • Sydney • Delhi

Cow

horns

Farmers milk their cows every day, so that we have fresh milk to drink. A baby cow is called a calf. A calf sucks milk from its mother's udder. Cows live out in the fields. They eat a lot of grass.

moo

cow

calf

7

Sheep

A mother
sheep is called
a ewe. A ewe has
her lambs in the
springtime. In early
summer farmers shear
their sheep. The winter
coats are spun into wool.

ewe

8

baa

tail

lamb

9

Chicken

A mother hen lays her eggs and sits on them to keep them warm. Fluffy yellow chicks hatch from the eggs after three weeks. The hen teaches her chicks to peck the ground to look for food.

cheep, cheep

chick

hen

11

Pig

A mother pig
is called a sow.
She has about
14 piglets at a

time. Some pigs live indoors in
a pigsty. Others are kept
outdoors. When it's hot,
they lie down
in wet mud
to keep cool.

oink, oink

sow

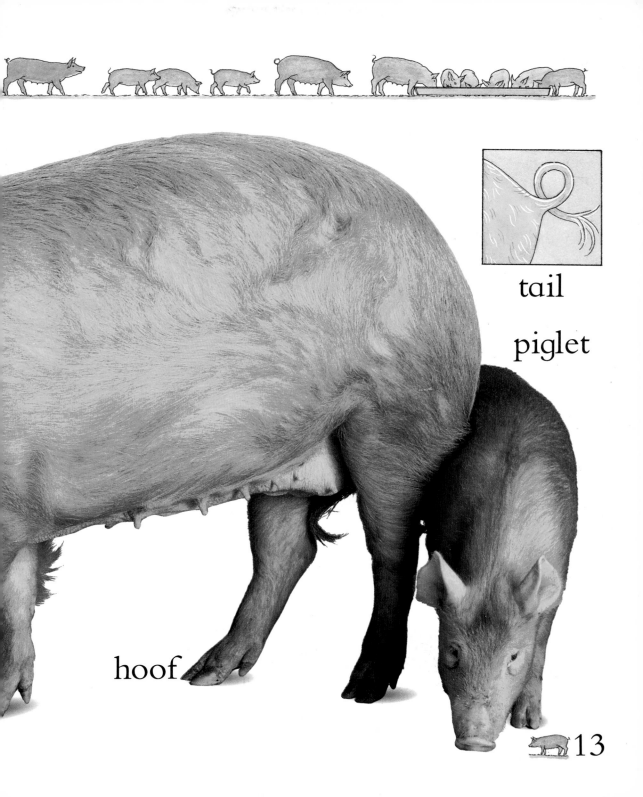

tail

piglet

hoof

13

Horse

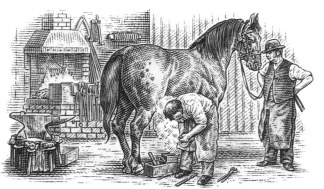

Some farmers keep work horses to pull heavy carts and machinery. Other farmers have horses for riding. A horse wears metal shoes to protect its hooves. A blacksmith nails on the shoes, but it does not hurt the horse.

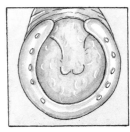

neigh

hoof

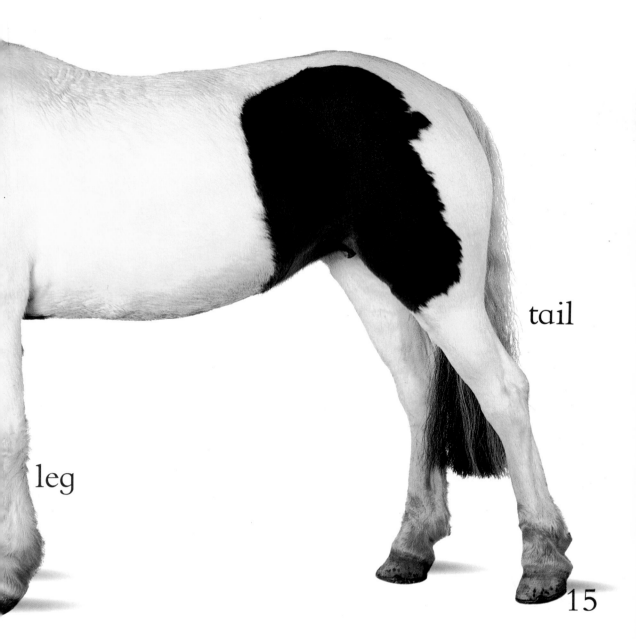

tail

leg

Duck

Ducks usually live near the farmyard pond or stream. They search for food in the water. Ducks eat worms, waterweeds, and seeds. A young duck is called a duckling.

ducklings

16

duck

foot

quack, quack

tail

17

Goat

A mother goat is called a nanny goat. Farmers milk their nanny goats. The milk is usually turned into cheese. Young goats are called kids. Kids playfully butt and chase each other around the fields.

nanny goat

beard

kid

meh, meh

udder

19

Sheepdog

Sheepdogs work hard for the farmer. They help round up sheep and other animals into pens. The dogs are trained to obey the farmer's calls and whistles.

ear

tail

paw

woof

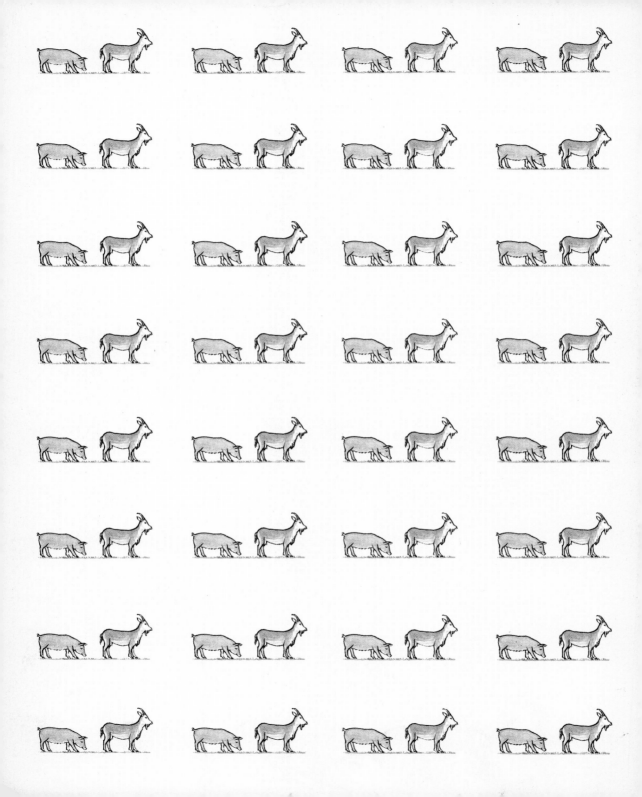

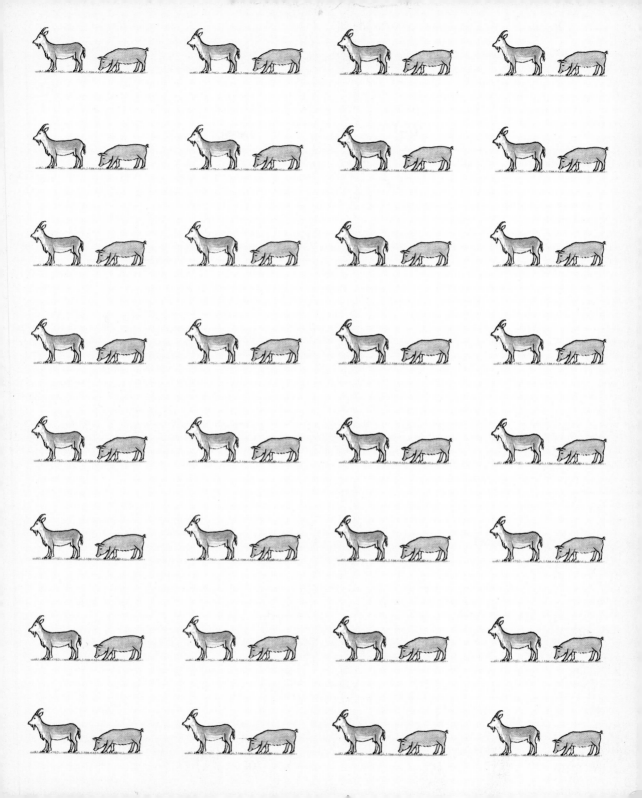